INTRODUCTION

The divine objective of this book is to provoke every believer to engage in spiritual warfare. The information in this book can be used as an excellent warfaring tool, especially for those who have been called, anointed, and appointed to engage in warfaring against the enemy of darkness. As you read and pray for divine insight, this book will motivate you to pray and navigate you to do battle against the enemy. It is essential for believers to recognize the demonic attacks that are assigned to man's three dimensional nature and the personalities of man. My book, which I give all glory to God will make a great impartation to all those who thirst for spiritual warfare, revelation and strategies. It is detailed with revelation knowledge, divinely given by God, to help promote and increase every believer with a greater insight into the spirit world. In the midst of conception and the birthing out of this book, I encountered pernicious and diabolical attacks against my life. Mentally the enemy tried to enforce a nervous breakdown upon me, physically I was experiencing manifestations of death, my facial appearance had transformed into my mother's face on her death bed. The spirit of Baalzebub was lingering around me waiting to collect my corpse. Because of the attacks, one morning I woke up and my heart was literally hurting. I was not having chest pains I felt like someone was holding my heart in their hand and squeezing it. But to the glory of God, no weapons formed against me prospered. This book has been birthed out of much suffering, pain, loneliness, and travailing, because of this unveiling. I do recommend that you purchase the fraternal twin to this book, my first release "Prayers for Spiritual Warfare" which has and still is blessing many lives. The name of God is to be glorified. Many blessings to all who have seeded into this ministry.

I do recommend before reading this book that you would cover yourself in prayer.

TABLE OF CONTENTS

Chapter 1:
    The Spirit World 13
    The Battleground 17
    Guerrilla Warfare 19
    Self-Realization 21

Chapter 2:
    God's Word 25
    Your Position 27
    Basic Training 33
    The Five Commandments of Satan 35
    The War Zone 37

Chapter 3:
    The Purpose of Spiritual Warfare 41
    Who is the Strongman? 45
    Where is the War Located? 49
    What type of Warfare is it? 51

Chapter 4:
    Three Personalities of Man 57
    Satan's Systematic Government 61

Chapter 5:
>Pre- Adamic Ancient Spirits..................................67

Chapter 6:
>Prayers.. 77-93

Chapter 1

The Spirit World

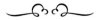

For which cause we faint not; but though our outward man perish, yet the inward man is renewed day by day.
                                    2 Corinthians 4:16

Each day we are deteriorating from this flesh world, and gaining access to the spirit world. When the fleshly aspect of man's three dimensional being demises, man returns back to his original state "a spirit". A spirit nature existing in a spirit world. In Genesis chapter one verses 26 and 27, God created the man and the woman in the spirit realm first. He made them in his image and his likeness. God then gave them dominion over the earth realm and He empowered them to replenish and subdue over every living thing that moveth upon the earth. The Spirit nature of man is the aspect of him that has been positioned, he is qualified, he has been given authority and power to take dominion and subdue things that are seen and unseen.

> And God said, Let us make man in our image, after our likeness: and let them have dominion over the fish of the sea, and over the fowl of the air, and over the cattle, and over all the earth, and over every creeping thing that creepth upon the earth.

> So God created man in his own image, in the image of God created he him; male and female created he them.
>
> Genesis 1:26-27

Genesis chapter two, is the place where God forms man in the earthly realm. Man which was created in the spirit realm first, is now being manifested into the natural realm. God now gives his spirit a earthly body to function, have dominion and subdue the earth world.

> And every plant of the field before it was in the earth, and every herb of the field before it grew: for the Lord God had not caused it to rain upon the earth, and there was not a man to till the ground.
> And the Lord God formed man of the dust of the ground, and breathed into his nostrils the breath of life; and man became a living soul.
>
> Genesis 2:5,7

We are a spirit being, cocooned within a body. The flesh nature is governed by the laws of nature according to this physical earth guidelines, that is mandated for the human or the flesh nature of him to exist and survive. The biological and physical needs according to the laws of Maslow for the human basic survival needs are: air, food, water, shelter, sex, warmth, sleep, health, and etc. These requirements must be met for human existence. The spirit world is the original world. It is alive and functioning, God the father, Jesus the son, and the Holy Spirit, angels, satan, demons, the spirit of man and all spiritual beings exist in the real world, which is spiritual. The vehicle to operate in the earthly realm, must be by possession of embodiment. Just as the Holy Spirit operates in mankind, the devil emulates the plans of God and assign his demons to also, operate in mankind. The world of the spirits had been in existence before this earthly world was spoken into existence by God. Jehovah is a spirit and a spirit does not consist of flesh and bones. After the resurrection of Jesus Christ he stated, in the book of Luke,

> "for a spirit hath not flesh and bones, as ye see me have".
>
> Luke 24:39b

The Battleground

For the believers, this natural world is not the target place where we fight the battle. Our warfare is to be fought in the spirit world. This world deals with the unseen eternal beings and their weapons. It is impossible to fight with carnal weapons and win the battle. Our weapons of warfare are: praying, fasting, the anointing, binding, loosening, intercessory, faith, love, forgiveness, the word of God, truth, gospel of salvation, releasing our angels, and obedience to the Holy Spirit.

> For though we walk in the flesh, we do not war after the flesh: (For the weapons of our warfare are not carnal, but mighty through God to the pulling down of strongholds;)
> Casting down imaginations, and every high thing that exalted itself against the knowledge of God, and bringing into captivity every thought to the obedience of Christ:
> 2 Corinthians 10:3-5

To engage in spiritual warfare, you must be educated in the rules of engagement, recognize your opponent, satan he is your enemy. Lucifer's systematic classes of demons are principalities, powers, rulers of darkness, spiritual wickedness in high places, dominion and thrones. Now is the time to become experienced in his tactics and his strategies. Have confidence that you are equipped and have been empowered by the Holy Ghost for the battle. Listen, in the natural military, there's a team called special operation's. This team is for special warriors, who has served in the past, present, and will serve in the future. You have been called to the team of special operations. You have served God in the past, present, and you will serve God in the future.

Guerrilla Warfare

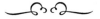

In order to defeat the enemy we must fight by all means necessary, that means to also, engage in guerrilla warfare. Guerrilla warfare is unconventional combat, which means you're not bound by no fixed rules or regulations. It's a small group of soldiers coming with surprise tactics, planning ambushes, raids and fighting as nasty as they want to be to win the battle. These soldiers keep pressure on the enemy, until it's diminished. We are warriors and we have been commissioned to demoralize the devil and take back our stuff.

It's time to become aggressive and hostile. We must become spiritually combative and fight. It is time to utilize every spiritual device and measure to overthrow the enemy.

> To every thing there is a season, and a time to every purpose under the heaven: A time of war, and a time of peace.
>
> Ecclesiastes 3:1,8b

Self-Realization

And from the days of John the Baptist until now the kingdom of heaven suffered violence, and the violent take it by force.
Matthew 11:12

It is of urgency to embrace who we are and walk in the power and authority that God has equipped us with. We are in a brutal warfare. The kingdom is losing souls, folks are compromising with the cares and the rudiments of this world. The world's system does not respect God, the things of God nor the people of God. We are constantly facing spiritual and physical brutality because of our faith in God.

Then shall they deliver you up to be afflicted, and shall kill you: and ye shall be hated of all nations for my name's sake.
Matthew 24:9

As soldiers, Jesus has enlisted us, and the Holy Ghost has equipped us for the battle. Hosea said, "My people perish because of a lack of knowledge." We must recognize who we are. Yes, Glory to God. We are redeemed people, who have been washed in the blood of the lamb. A new creature with the attributes of Christ. Now give God a praise, right there.

Minister to yourself; in other words encourage yourself. Tell yourself that it is imperative that I recognize that old person in me is now dead. He is powerless and has no authority over me. I am a brand new creature, positioned in a fresh regenerated state because of the transformation (the new birth). I embrace power, authority, and benefits.

> Therefore if any man be in Christ, he is a new creature: old things are passed away: behold, all things are become new.
> 2 Corinthians 5:16

> Verily I say unto you, whatsoever ye shall bind on earth shall be bound in heaven: and whatever ye shall loose on earth shall be loosed in heaven.
> Matthew 18:18

> Behold, I give unto you power to tread on serpents and scorpions, and over all the power of the enemy: and nothing shall by any means hurt you.
> Luke 10:19

Chapter 2

God's Word

If you desire to warfare and obtain results, it is vital to understand the power and the laws of God's word. God's word is like a living organism: it's alive, it creates, it causes things to happen. God's word cannot fail. Jesus confirms this in Luke the sixteenth chapter. He said "And it is easier for heaven and earth to pass, than one tittle of the law to fail". God's promises is a legally binding contract that gives the believer the right to expect or declare specific acts. God cannot lie and his word is true.

> In hope of eternal life, which God, that cannot lie, promised before the world began;
> Titus 1:2

> Sanctify them through thy truth: thy word is truth.
> John 17:17

Once the word is released with faith, it has been activated to make something happen. Remember the word is spirit, it is activated in the spirit realm first and then the word becomes alive in the natural realm. Warfaring with God's word will give you the victory in your battles. The moment the word of God becomes alive in your spirit, speak the word and confess the word in faith.

> So shall my word be that goeth forth out of my mouth: it shall not return unto me void, but it shall accomplish that which I please, and it shall prosper in the thing whereto I sent it.
> Isaiah 55:11

God created by speaking words. In Genesis, God spoke the elements, the animal kingdom, the plant kingdom, and everything into existence. As new creatures in Christ, we also have the ability to create by speaking the word of God. In Matthew, Jesus validates the spoken word of God.

> But he answered and said, It is written, man shall not live by bread alone, but by every word that proceedth out of the mouth of God.
> Matthew 4:4

> Death and life are in the power of the tongue:
> Proverbs 18:21

As a new creature, created in God's image, we can release either words of life or words of death. We have the authority to bind and loose. As you meditate on God's word, faith will leap into your Spirit. Now, you can boldly declare what God has spoken in His word.

Your Position

> And from the days of John the Baptist until now the kingdom of heaven suffered violence, and the violent take it by force.
>
> Matthew 11:12

In describing our position as fighters, it is essential that we view ourselves as a policeman, a wrestler, a boxer, and a soldier. Recognize that you have been positioned to do battle and you have been empowered to meet the challenge of warfaring for the kingdom of righteousness. Greater is God (Jehovah the omnipotent one) that is in you, than he that is of the world. Know that you have been equipped for the battle.

A Policeman

We have the authority and the backup to enforce the spiritual laws, regarding spiritual warfare as a policeman. We have been strategically planted in our walk with God, to enforce the law of righteousness by placing handcuffs on the enemy through binding and loosing. Anything that comes against the laws of God's plan for mankind, we can arrest it, placing handcuffs on it, which is the process of binding the demonic forces, that has broken the laws and order of God. After binding the strongman, the producer of the crime, you are now in position to victimize or sabotage his manifestations.

> Or else how can one enter into a strong man's house, and spoil his goods, except he first bind the strongman and then he will spoil his house.
> Matthew 12:29

A Wrestler

As believers, our target place to fight the battle is in the spirit realm. The devil has a systematic strategic plan for wrestling with the righteous ones of God. As a wrestler, your battle may sometimes be with principalities (the low level demons that rules territories). You may find yourself wrestling with powers (this system is the mitochondria to the demonic forces, empowering them). As wrestlers we all encounter the strongman, rulers we have the authority to pin him down. To wrestle with spiritual wickedness in high places, God has equipped the believers to go into strategic level warfare. Now this is a place whereas we can give charge to our ministering angels, to assist us in battle. (read Daniel 10)

> For we wrestle not against flesh and blood, but against principalities, against powers, against the rulers of the darkness of this world, against spiritual wickedness in high places.
> Ephesians 6:12

A Boxer

Your position in fighting the battle, do not fight with uncertainness. You must know, that you know, that you are equipped for the battle. David said, thy word have I hid in my heart, so that I may not sin against thee. The word is, you can do all things through Christ who strengthens you. The word is, if God be for me, who can be against me. Know that you are more than a conqueror through Christ Jesus. As a boxer don't box with doubt, box with certainty.

> I therefore so run, not as uncertainly: so fight I not as one that beateth the air.
> 1 Corinthians 9:26

When satan approaches you in a situation, give him a double-blow by giving him the word Jesus said:

> It is written, Man shall not live by bread alone, but by every word that proceeded out of the mouth of God.
> Matthew 4:4

Give the enemy a double-blow with the promises of what the word of God says. If you have been hit by fear, give a double blow of the word of God. Fear will cause you to stagger and not produce faith.

> For God hath not given us the spirit of fear; but of power, and of love, and of a sound mind.
> 2 Timothy 1:7

Satan does not know how to fight fair. Therefore, when you receive a punch below the belt with an infirmity then you must fight back with the word of God and declare that you are healed in Jesus' name.

> Behold, I will bring it health and cure, and I will cure them, and will reveal unto them the abundance of peace and truth.
>
> Jeremiah 33:6

Many times in our Christian walk we may receive a blow to the chest which will knock the wind out of us such as pernicious trial, tribulation, and calamity. Due to these circumstances, you may find yourself in a weakened state. Encourage yourself that you can stand, just abide in the promises of God's word.

> Fear thou not; for I am with thee: be not dismayed; for I am thy God: I will strengthen thee; yea, I will help thee; yea, I will uphold thee with the right hand of my righteousness.
>
> Isaiah 41:10

As a boxer, you will find yourself sometimes in the face of the enemy and may receive an upper cut. During those times it may seem as though you have been overtaken, but the fight is not over yet. Know that God will lift up a standard against the enemy and you are a overcomer by the blood of the Lamb.

> When the enemy shall come in like a flood, the spirit of the Lord shall lift up a standard against him.
>
> Isaiah 59:19b

Do not waver from the promises of God, box with focus, do not become distracted from the promise. Don't doubt. We walk by faith and not by sight.

But let him ask in faith, nothing wavering, for he that wavereth is like a wave of the sea driven with the wind and tossed.
James 1:6

If you fight with the promises in your battle, you are fighting under the dunamis of the holy spirit that will give you the victory. Don't just knock the enemy down, knock him out!

A Soldier

This is a spiritual warfare and God has enlisted you for the battle. Endure hardness as a good soldier. Put on your army fatigues (the armour of God) and stand against the wiles of the devil. God needs folks who will fight the battle and not look for extra benefits, extra recognition, and folks who refuse to prostitute their gifts. God needs soldiers who will do the task they are assigned to do. Folks that will be deployed to where they are assigned to do battle. The kingdom of God need warriors that are committed and will walk away with an honorable discharge that signifies, well done my good and faithful servant. You have been faithful over a few things, now I will make you rulers over many.

Thou therefore endure hardness, as a good soldier of Jesus Christ.
2 Timothy 2:3

Basic Training

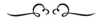

There is an urgency for kingdom men and women to be drafted into spiritual warfare. We are living in perilous times. The death rate has increased among children, women, and men. The death spirit Sam(m)uel and the spirit of Manasseh is permeating through the land. He that hath an ear let him hear what the spirit of God is saying to the church. The spirit of Leviathan has invaded the church with spiritual pride. The demon Orion is promoting spiritual death to deliverance ministries. The kingdom is in need of warfare and prophetic intercessors that can prophetically stop the premature acts of the spirit of the red horse.

> And there went out another horse that was red: and power was given to him that sat thereon to take peace from the earth, and that they should kill one another: and there was given unto him a great sword.
>
> Revelation 6:4

The chief demonic angel Abaddon (destruction), which abides in the bottomless pit, is now manifesting his evil demonic activities through existing demons such as rulers and principalities, which are manifesting their evil deeds in the hearts of men.

And they had a king over them, which is the angel of the bottomless pit, whose name in the Hebrew tongue is Abaddon, but in the Greek tongue hath his name Apollyon.

Revelation 9:11

Again, I declare in the spirit there is a code blue alert. The kingdom of God is in need of men, women, and youth to enlist and survive military training, soldiers who will proclaim, "I don't mind lying down my life for God's kingdom". It may not feel good, I may be uncomfortable or I even may be walking wounded. Regardless it is imperative that we defend the kingdom of God. Encourage yourself, you will survive basic training. Tell the enemy, you refuse to be kool-aid (killed in action), because no weapons formed against you shall prosper.

The kingdom is not in need of phony looking and phony acting soldiers. These are honey-dippers, a soldier that is responsible for burning human dung. It's time to do battle and go into Guerrilla warfare utilizing camouflage to capture the occult, the wiles and every weapon of the enemy. The war is on, transform your mind. Do not go into battle as a boot soldier with an expectant mentality, (a casualty that is expected to die). Strengthen your mind. You shall live and not die, but declare the works of God. There is no time to be Diddy-bopping (walking carelessly). It's now, time to fight and endure hardness as a good soldier.

The Five Commandments of Satan

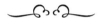

As I stated earlier, Satan's plan is to emulate the plans and the order of God, but in a diabolical way. Just as God gave his commandments, Lucifer also stated his commandments. In the book of Isaiah 14 chapter is noted the devil's five commandments:

(1) I will ascend to heaven.
(2) I will raise my throne above the stars of God.
(3) I will sit on the mount of the assembly in the recesses of the north.
(4) I will ascend above the heights of the clouds.
(5) I will make myself like the most high.

When Lucifer made warfare with God in heaven this sin was heinous and caused a pernicious widespread effect upon God's creation. Satan's sin affected other angels.

> And there was war in heaven; Michael and his angels fought against the dragon, and the dragon fought and his angels.
>
> Revelation 12:7

Satan's sin affected all mankind and nations. It also positioned him as the ruler of this world and the prince of the air.

> Wherein in time past ye walked according to the course of this world, according to the prince of the air, the spirit that now worketh in the children of disobedience.
>
> Ephesians 2:2

Praise God, He gave his only begotten Son, so that we may have eternal life. Jesus Christ the anointed one came that we might have life, and that we might have it more abundantly. The battle had been won over two thousand years ago.

The War Zone

At times, you may find yourself in the kill zone, the enemy will plant an explosive device to take you out, because he knows you are anointed and can cause danger to his kingdom, but you can counteract with your AK 47.

> The Lord has given me power to tread on serpents and scorpions, and over all the power of the enemy; and nothing shall by any means hurt me.
> Luke 10:19

> Many are the afflictions of the righteous but my God shall deliver us out of the them all.
> Psalm 37:19

The enemy is walking around like a lion, with his comrades strategically positioned. The devil has set his perimeters for the battle. Now, it's time for us, the believers to rock and roll. Put our weapons on full automatic and speak every word that proceeded out of the mouth of God. Oh yes, the devil has set up spider holes (this is a camouflaged fox hole). His purpose is for you to fall and become entrapped. Be prayerful, be alert, know that you're able to stand against the wiles of the devil.

Don't be branded as a peanut (always wounded in action). Don't be easily offended and that everything hurts your feelings and now, you want to quit the battle. When the kingdom is being challenged, Jesus don't need POW's (prisoners of war), MIA's (missing in action) or believers going Awol (absent without leave). The Lord has empowered you to fight the good fight of faith. Jesus never said it was going to always be easy; no cross, no crown.

> Thou therefore endure hardness, as a good soldier of Jesus Christ.
>
> 1 Timothy 6:12

> No man that warreth entangleth himself with the affairs of this life; that he may place him who hath chosen him to be a soldier.
>
> 2 Timothy 2:4

Chapter 3

The Purpose of Spiritual Warfare

Demonic forces that is operating in darkness, are constantly fighting to defeat the righteous and overthrow our faith in God. 1 Timothy 6:12, encourages the believers to fight the good fight of faith. There is an urgency for the believers to fight, because we are in Holy warfare, the devil is determined to victimize and put the people of God in bondage.

Satan has a Purpose

To win the battle you must know your enemy. Well, it is imperative that the people of God, know that satan plans his attacks. He has a strategy in every situation. He is intelligent and diabolical. The devil has a systematic order, he tries to emulate the plan and order of God in pernicious ways. Satan is a counterfeiter and he is constantly promoting the opposite of God.

The devil implements his strategies, through temptation and wiles. Temptation is being in a state to be tempted or something that tempts you. Temptation targets the areas, that has always defeated you in the past. In other words you know the areas in your life that is vulnerable to sin. Apostle Peter instructs us to be alert, be on guard. Demons want to devour us, our marriages, children, ministries, finances, health, etc. The purpose of temptations is to make you rebel and sin. It will harden your heart against the things of God. And finally, to terminate you from your purpose and the will of God.

> Be sober, be vigilant; because your adversary the devil, as a roaring lion, walketh about, seeking whom he may devour:
> 1 Peter 5:8

The second strategy is wiles, wiles is a crafty trick or subtle words, that is intended to deceive or lure and to move the people of God into sin by trickery. This scheme is hidden, it is the occult and not obvious like a temptation. The purpose of a wile is to lure you or deceive you, to rebel and sin against God. Wiles come to harden your heart against the things of God. And finally, to terminate you from your destiny and the will of God.

> Put on the whole armour of God, that ye may be able to stand against the wiles of the devil.
> Ephesians 6:11

As Christians we are mandated to engage in spiritual warfare. We have been given a spiritual responsibility to cast down anything that exalts itself above the knowledge of God's will and purpose for us. The nature of mankind is in a crisis, folks are being consumed by immorality, sexual perversion, and lawlessness.

> For though we walk in the flesh, we do not war after the flesh. For the weapons of our warfare are not carnal, but mighty through God to the pulling down of strongholds, casting down imaginations, and

everything that exalted itself against the knowledge of God, and bringing into captivity every thought to the obedience of Christ.

2 Corinthians 10:3-5

Who is the Strongman?

To engage in warfare, there are three principles you must know. One, who is the strongman? Two, where is the war located? Is it body, soul, or spirit. And three, what type of warfare is it? It is ground, occult, or strategic level. In conducting spiritual warfare, you must purpose not to be a novice. Educate yourself, become empowered in the Holy Ghost and equip yourself for the battle. In warfaring against satan, be knowledgeable of his defense measures and be in position to counteract them.

First, recognize who is the strongman, the ruling demon according to Matthew 12:29; The ruling demon is the one who has jurisdiction over that vessel that has been enslaved. Jurisdiction means a lawful right to govern, having authority or control. Remember, the devil has a legal right to dwell in any area of darkness within our life. Do not give him legal rights to dwell in your life. For God said, I will not dwell in no unclean vessel.

> Or else how can one enter into a strong man's house and spoil his goods, except he first bind the strong man? And then he will spoil his house.
> Matthew 12:29

Here is a list of some ruling demons, known as the strongman.

Spirit of divination	Dumb and Deaf Spirit
Spirit of Jealousy	Spirit of Infirmity
Spirit of Anti-Christ	Lying Spirit
Spirit of Error	Spirit of Korah
Spirit of Haughtiness	Python Spirit
Spirit of Bondage	Spirit of Idolatory
Spirit of Fear	Spirit of Sam(m)uel
Spirit of Amnon	Spirit of Perversion
Spirit of Gomer	Spirit of Jezebel
Spirit of Heaviness	Spirit of Cain
Spirit of Hulda	Spirit of Leviathan
Spirit of Succubus	Spirit of Orion
Spirit of Incubus	Spirit of Mammon
Spirit of Manasseh	Spirit of the World
Spirit of Tamar	Spirit of the Power of the Air
Spirit of Belphegor	Spirit of Baalzebub
Spirit of Azazel	Spirit of Behemoth

Rulers of darkness are the ruling demons.

For we wrestle not against flesh and blood, but against principalities, against powers, against the rulers of the darkness of this world, against spiritual wickedness in high places.

Ephesians 6:12

To recognize the strongman, you must do some spiritual diagnosing. You must be alert to his signs and symptoms, which are manifestations. When a person goes to the doctor because he or she may suspect that they are having a heart attack, that person will give the doctor their signs and symptoms.

Some symptoms maybe chest pain, pain radiating to the left arm with tingling, shortness of breath, skin clammy, and feeling nauseated. The strongman here is heart attack and the manifestation are the signs and symptoms.

(1) Example of a strongman is the Spirit of Fear. The manifestation which are the signs and symptoms are: torment, horror, fright, anxiety, stress, untrusting, nightmares, shy, worry, and terror.
(2) Example of a strongman is the Spirit of Haughtiness. The manifestations are: pride, scornful, self-righteousness, egotistic, stiff-necked, lofty looks, arrogant, vanity, and exalted feelings.
(3) Example of a strongman is the Spirit of Delilah. Her manifestations are: deceitful, seductive, cold hearted, out for personal gain, liar, and causes a man's relationship to deteriorate from God, his marriage, and family.
(4) Example of a strongman is the Python Spirit. This spirit is associated with the spirit of divination. His manifestations are: it causes natural and spiritual constriction, it squeezes, limits mobility, it tightens and apply pressure. It limits progress in ministry. It causes natural and spiritual asphyxiation, it crushes and kills.
(5) Example of a strongman is the Spirit of Haman. He sends a death assignment to family members and a nationality of people. His manifestations are: anger, retaliation, bitterness, unforgiving, arrogance, enraged, desires to kill the family or a race of people, persuasion, destruction, murder, to annihilate and to massacre.
(6) Example of a strongman is the Spirit of Perversion. His manifestations are: lust, prostitution, homosexuality, incest, rebellion, fornication, exposure, adul-

tery, pornography, error, filthy mind, pedifile, rape, and transvestite.

(7) Example of a strongman is the Spirit of Korah. This diabolic spirit operates among the ministerial and priestly calling. A minister who tries to undermine spiritual authority within the congregation. His manifestations are: Rebellion, not satisfied with his/her position in the church, wants to be the spiritual authority in the church, oversteps his/her boundary, rejects the pastor, brings spiritual division in the church, encourages part of the congregation to follow their leadership. They are power hungry and envious.

Where is the War located?

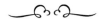

Not all physical and mental infirmities are medically prompt, some illnesses may be demonically induced. Man is a three dimensional being. He is body, soul, and spirit. His body was created from the dust by God. Demons can oppress and possess the body. Some strongmen that targets the body are: spirit of infirmity, dumb and deaf, perversion, spirit of Delilah, spirit of bondage, spirit of gomer and spirit of divination.

Man received the breath of God, which made him a living soul. (Genesis 2:7) In man's soulish realm, it houses five entities which are: will, emotions, intellect, memory, and his imagination. Demons will attack and can be assigned to these areas. Some strongmen are: spirit of heaviness, spirit of fear, schizophrenia, phobias, rejection, lying spirit, covetousness, error, jealousy, illiteracy, suicidal, stubbornness, rebellion, amnesia, and jezebel. The Spirit of divination can enslave the five entities of the soulish realm, the body and the spirit man.

The spirit of heaviness, the assigned demon targets the victim's emotions, binding him with demonic manifestations of depression, sadness, despair, discouragement, gloominess, hopelessness, suicide, and etc. Some other demons that attack the emotions are spirit of fear, perversion, haughtiness, jealousy, spider spirit, and some mental infirmities.

The spirit of schizophrenia, spirit of lying, the snake spirit and spirit of phobias attack the imagination.

The deaf and dumb spirit, spirit of error, owl spirit, spirit of illiteracy are demonic spirits that attack the intellect.

Demons of amnesia, and forgetfulness targets the memory.

The Spirit of rebellion, the spirit of death, spirit of bondage and the turtle spirit, the bat spirit, spirit of the world, all attack the will of man.

Man also have a spirit, which was made in God's image (Genesis 1:26). Demonic spirits can attack and possess his spirit. These strongmen are: gaynism, lesbianism, effeminate, bestiality, bat spirit, blocking spirit, bondage, jezebel, anti-Christ, athaliah, and giantism.

What Type of Warfare is it?

Before engaging in spiritual warfare, you must recognize there are three levels of spiritual warfare. In other words there are three locations where the battle is to be fought. The place of warfaring is either ground level, occult level, or strategic level. Know the type of war you are going to engage in. In the natural, we have different types of warfare. Just to name a few, chemical warfare, biological warfare, psychological warfare, and Guerilla warfare.

Ground Level Warfare

This is the most frequent foundational level of spiritual warfare most believers engage in and is most familiar with. Some examples of ground level warfare are: spirit of jealousy, spirit of error, perverse spirit, spirit of haughtiness, spirit of bondage, lying spirit, spirit of fear, dumb and deaf spirit, spirit of infirmity, spirit of Delilah, spirit of Jericho, succubus spirit, incubus spirit, and the spirit of bestiality. Jesus did ground level warfare, when he casted out the dumb and deaf spirit in a child in the book of Mark.

> When Jesus saw that the people came running together, he rebuked the foul spirit, saying unto him,

> thou dumb and deaf spirit, I charge thee, come out of him, and enter no more into him.
>
> Mark 9:25

The dumb and deaf spirit is the strongman ruling today's young people. This spirit is producing sickness, destruction, and death. It robs them from speaking the righteousness of God and silence their ears to the gospel of salvation.

Occult Level Warfare

Occult means hidden. This type of warfare deals with the unseen, or the supernatural. It involves divination, spells, curses, fortune telling, occultism, satanic priests, witches, warlocks, and etc. Some examples of occult level warfare are: spirit of Divination, Jezebel spirit, spirit of death, python spirit, spirit of leviathan, spirit of hulda, spirit of Manasseh, spirit of belial, spirit of azazel, spirit of behemoth, succubus spirit, and incubus spirit. Apostle Paul engaged in occult level warfare, when he commanded the spirit of divination to come out of the damsel in the book of Acts 16th chapter.

> And it came to pass, as we went to prayer, a certain damsel possessed with a spirit of divination met us, which brought her masters much gain by soothsaying: The same followed Paul and us, and cried, saying, these men are the servants of the most high God, which show unto us the way of salvation. And this did she many days, but Paul, being grieved, torn, and said to the spirit, I command thee in the name of Jesus Christ to come out of her, and she came out the same hour.
>
> Acts 16:16-18

Strategic Level Warfare

This is warfare at the highest level. Dealing with territorial, principalities and powers. Engaging in war in the heavenlies, affecting cities, government, regions, communities, nations, international, and global territories. Some examples of strategic level warfare are: spirit of anti-christ, spirit of Babylon, spirit of Athaliah, spirit of Babel, spirit of Nimrod, the spirit of the power of the air, spirit of Haman, the spirit of the world. In Daniel 10th chapter defines strategic level warfare.

> Then said he unto me, fear not, Daniel: for from the first day that thou didst set thine heart to understand, and to chasten thyself before thy God, thy words were heard, and I am come for thy words. But the prince of the kingdom of Persia withstood me one and twenty days: but, lo, Michael, one of the chief princes, came to help me: and I remained there with the kings of Persia.
>
> Daniel 10:12-13

Chapter 4

Three Personalities of Man

Personality is the dynamic that governs an individual's cognitive drive and it's behaviors. It embraces the way a person thinks, reacts, feels, attitudes, moods, and their social interactions skills. Demons can also oppress and possess the personality of man. Some mental health infirmities maybe induced by a demonic origin. The bible clearly informs us that there is nothing new up under the sun. I often quote, how is it in biblical times people could recognize a demon in operation from a mental health issue. Often our children are diagnosed with mental health issues. Ask yourself, is it biological or is there demonic influence? In Mark 9th chapter, the father recognized his son had a demon, instead of a mental health issue. The bible clearly states, the father took his son to Jesus and openly acknowledged that his son had an unclean spirit.

> And one of the multitude answered and said, master, I have brought unto thee my son, which hath a dumb spirit.
> Mark 9:17

Also, in Mark 7th chapter, a Greek mother recognized that her daughter had an unclean spirit. This mother brought her child to Jesus to have the demon cast out. In today's society, many of our children and adults are oppressed and possessed by demonic activity that is controlling their id, ego, and superego.

> For a certain woman, whose young daughter had an unclean spirit, heard of him, and came and fell at his feet: The woman was a Greek, a Syrophenician by nation: and she besought him that he would cast forth the devil out of her daughter.
>
> Mark 7:25-26

This war can also be located in the three personalities of man. His id, ego, and superego. Demons strive to invade and possess every aspect of man's nature and personality. Demonic possession of the personality can manifest selfishness, all types of sexual perversion, apathy, effeminate man, masculine woman, serial killers, mass murderers, pedophiles, schizophrenias, bipolar disorders, paranoias, narcissistic disorders (excessive importance of oneself), antisocial disorders (this behavior can be criminal, it exploits and violates others), histrionic disorders (excessive attention seekers), and obsessive compulsive personality.

In the book of Mark 5th chapter, an unclean spirit possessed a man's personality. The demons controlled his thought process, his reaction, his attitude, his mood, feelings, and his social skills. The demonic spirits had complete control of this man's personality. First of all he thought he had to dwell among the dead, in a graveyard. This man could not interact with society. The demons controlled his reaction, he was violent and would cut himself, also the demons controlled his feelings and attitude. He was depressed and always crying. Many folks today, especially our youth have opened the door of dwelling among the dead. Promoting logos that relate to death on clothing, jewelry, music, and even their bodies.

ID

The id is the pleasure seeking aspect of the personality. It desires instant gratification. The id thrives for instant satisfaction of bodily needs. The spirit of whoredom possessed Samson's id. He was controlled by sexual sins which gave him instant gratification because his personality was demon controlled, he desecrated the Nazareth vows in his life. He did not respect the anointing that God embraced him with, and finally he toyed with the anointing and lost his strength.

Superego

Within the superego, there are two components; the conscience and the ego-ideal. The conscience is where we have the ability to feel and understand. It contains our prohibition and our restriction, preventing man's conscience from doing certain things. The ego-ideal contains man's aspirations and values that he or she strive for.

The spirit of rebellion possessed Saul's superego. In 1 Samuel 13 chapter King Saul offered a sacrificial offering contrary to God's word. The demon in him provoked him and Saul was not restrained from operating in the priestly realm of performing burnt offering, which only the priest could perform. Folks that are neurotic, mass murderers (serial killers), sociopaths, pedophiles, and rapist exhibit demonic spirits that may have processed their superego's. This is the reason they have no restrictions to what is morally right.

EGO

The ego is the reality component of the personality. It controls our desires and expresses them in appropriate ways. The spirit of haughtiness possessed Peter's ego, when he got beside himself and rebuked Jesus in Matthew 16:21-23.

(21) From that time forth Jesus began to show unto his disciples, how that he must go unto Jerusalem, and suffer many things of the elders and chief priests and scribes, and be killed, and be raised again the third day.
(22) Then Peter took him, and began to rebuke him, saying, Be it far from thee, Lord: this shall not be unto thee.
(23) But he turned, and said unto Peter, Get thee behind me, Satan: thou art an offence unto me: for thou savourest not the things that be of God, but those that be of men.

Satan's Systematic Government

> For we wrestle not against flesh and blood, but against principalities, against powers, against rulers of the darkness of this world, against spiritual wickedness in high places.
>
> Ephesians 6:12

The Apostle Paul was continuously battling spiritual conflicts with satan and his demons. Here in the book of Ephesians, he unveils the devil governmental system. I remember when the Holy Spirit gave me this revelation, it was in the late 1980's. I taught this revelation one Friday night in our prayer band meeting. The next day my children and I was in a near fatal accident. I thank God, for the spirit of Protection because I could feel the angels embracing us in the car. Listen, satan is not omnipresent, so his plan of attack must be organized and structured.

Class One

Principalities, are the lower class of demons that do little thinking and decision making. They are dictated to and obey the commands of rulers of darkness. They are busy carrying out demonic assignments. Principalities mimic the ministering angels of God. I have seen their appearance in the spirit realm. They are normally black and have a type of monkey like or animal formation.

Class Two

The second demonic class is Powers. Powers are like the mitochondria of satan's governmental system. They equip and empower other demons with authority to do evil. They are the power suppliers. These demons equips and gives authority to principalities and rulers. As I stated earlier the devil emulates the plan of God. Power demons mimic the Holy Ghost. They are limited, but they possess intelligence, emotions, and they can express their wills. Power demons are combative, will cause mockery, resistance and will cause danger, especially to the victim. Powers can permeate or transfer from the spiritual realm to the natural realm of mankind or into animals bodies. Power demons increases the force and help energize the manifestation of the ruling demon (the strongman).

> (29) For he had commanded the unclean spirit to come out of the man. For often times it had caught him: and he was kept bound with chains and in fetters: and he brake the bands, and was driven of the devil into the wilderness.
> (30) And Jesus asked him, saying, what is thy name? And he said, legion: because many devils were entered into him.
> (31) And they besought him that he would not command them to go out into the deep.
> (32) And there was there a herd of many swine feeding on the mountain: and they besought him that he would suffer them to enter into them. And he suffered them.

(33) Then went the devils out of the man, and entered into the swine: and the herd ran violently down a steep place into the lake, and were choked.

Luke 8:29-33

One Friday night, many years ago we were in our prayer band meeting, one of the members there was possessed with the spirit of divination, she was under the influence of power demons. That night I was led to pray for her and as I stood before her, I could feel a supernatural antagonistic force. There were many demons standing in front of her. They were black, large and closely linked together, clawing at me. I laid hands on her in Jesus name; she fell to the floor and several power demons began to cry out of her. Remember, they are intelligent. When she got up, she was not completely delivered. The power demons instructed her to leave, before she could receive her full deliverance.

Class Three

Rulers are the third class of demons, and is known as the strongman. He is the advocate to rule, meaning to guide and control actions or behaviors. Ruler demons are the ones who governs or reigns. When Jesus rose he had all power in his authority. He governs and rules. Ruler demons mimic Jesus, the son of the living God. Rulers are the strongmen that are assigned over individuals, families, territorial, geographical areas, geo-political areas, churches and etc. Jesus gave the believers power to bind the strongman and to spoil his house (principalities and powers).

The demons (legion) was the demons of principalities and powers. In Luke 8 chapter the demon principalities and powers were following the instruction given to them by rulers. The man of Gadarenes was possessed with many demons. Jesus asked him (single) what is thy name? He did not ask for all the demons name. Jesus spoke directly to the ruler of darkness, the strongman.

Class Four

Spiritual wickedness in high places, is satan himself. His last commandment was, "I will be like the most High". In his commandment, he revealed his plan was to emulate God. The devil is known as the "Prince of the power of the air".

> Wherein in the time past ye walked according to the course of this world, according to the Prince of the power of the air, the spirit that now worketh in the children of disobedience:
> Ephesians 2:2

Chapter 5

Pre-Adamic Ancient Spirits

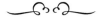

In the month of April 2008, as I was in prayer. God spoke to me and said, pray against the death spirit that is lingering in the occult and strategically over South Florida. There is a demonic assignment to exterminate a population of young people. Also, there is a hidden pernicious assignment to destroy those that are anointed and called by God to keep them from walking and fulfilling their purpose and destiny. The devil has assigned the spirit of premature death to abort the people of God's mission. These death spirits such as Sam(m)ael and Azrael are ancient pre-adamic fallen demons which are assigned to bring death to mankind. Sam(m)ael and Azrael have camouflaged themselves from the beginning of time. Many of the Bible characters and idol gods has been embodied by these demons. King Manasseh practice child sacrifice. Chemosh an idol god of the Moabites and Molech an idol god of the ammonite practice child sacrifice. Haman tried to exterminate the Jewish nation, and Hitler killed many Jews. These folks were possessed by these ancient pre-adamic fallen death demons Sam(m)uel and Azrael. Demons need to be embodied, rather it be people, objects, animals, or situations to operate, and promote their evil deeds. Demons are spirits and they are immaterial.

King Manasseh

And he made his son pass through the fire, and observed the times, and used enchantments, and dealt with familiar spirits and wizards: he wrought much wickedness in the sight of the Lord, to provoke him to anger.

2 Kings 21:6

Idol god Chemosh

And when the king of Moab saw that the battle was too sore for him, he took with him seven hundred men that drew swords, to break through even unto the king of Edom: but they could not.

Then he took his eldest son that should have reigned in his stead, and offered him for a burnt offering upon the wall. And there was great indignation against Israel: and they departed from him, and returned to their own land.

2 Kings 3:27

Idol god Molech

And thou shalt not let any of thy seed pass through the fire to Molech, neither shalt thou profane the name of thy God: I am the Lord.

Leviticus 18:21

Listen, to every thing there is a name. Look at the single cell animals (protozoa, ameoba) that can not be seen with the natural eye. These single cell creatures have a name. Every angel and every fallen angel (which are demons) have a name.

And out of the ground the Lord God formed every beast of the field, and every fowl of the air; and brought then unto Adam to see what he would call them: And whatsoever Adam called every living creature, that was the name thereof.
Genesis 2:19

Sexually Perverted Demons

Belphegor is one of the pre-adamic fallen angels that fell with Lucifer from heaven. He promotes all types of sexual perversion such as orgies, swingers, child prostitution, sex slavery, menageatrois, pornography, and gang-rape. He disguised himself as a beautiful naked woman or a demon with horns, pointed ears, long pointed nose, open mouth, long pointed fingers, and toes with long nails and a long tail. God told Israel that he was going to bless them to dwell in Canaan, the land of milk and honey, but to avoid association with the pagan worshippers. These pagan worshippers were into worshipping Pre-adamic ancient demons that had disguised themselves in the form of many idol images. This is the reason why God was so intense and specific regarding the Isrealites being separated from the pagans because of their religion and idols were infested with demons.

Thou shalt not bow down to their gods, nor serve them, nor do after their works: but thou shalt utterly overthrow them, and quite break down their images.
Exodus 23:24

Ye shall make you no idols nor graven image, neither rear you up a standing image, neither shall ye set up any image of stone in your land, to bow down unto it: for I am the Lord your God.
Leviticus 26:1

That same principle applies today, to us as believers, God instructs us to come out from among them and touch not the unclean things. In todays, society there are demonic activities that operates in certain music, certain television programs, certain cartoons, idols, creatures of the night, certain movies, tattoos, body piercing, demonic games, figurines of demon gods, Occultic drawing or pictures, hand carved objects, jewelry and paraphernalia from heathen cultures, certain fashions (skull head) and other demonic related images.

> For I will deliver the inhabitants of the land into your hand; and thou shalt drive them out before thee. Thou shalt make no covenant with them, nor with their gods. They shall not dwell in thy land, lest they make thee sin against me: for if thou serve their gods, it will surely be a snare unto thee.
>
> Exodus 23:31b - 33

> Take heed to thyself, lest thou make a covenant with the inhabitants of the land whither thou goest, lest it be for a snare in the midst of thee: But ye shall destory their altars, break their images, and cut down their groves: For thou shalt worship no other god: for the Lord, whose name is Jealous, is a jealous God: Lest thou make a covenant with the inhabitants of the land, and they go a whoring after their gods, and do sacrifice unto their gods, and one call thee, and thou eat of his sacrifice; And thou take of their daughters unto thy sons, and their daughters go a-whoring after their gods, and make thy sons go a-whoring after their gods. Thou shalt make thee no molten gods.
>
> Exodus 34:12 - 17

Wherefore come out from among them, and be ye separate, saith the Lord, and touch not the unclean thing; and I will receive you,
2 Corinthians 6:17

In the book of Numbers 25th chapter. The Moabites worshipped Belphegor his disguise was an idol image of a phallus (image of a penis) and his name was Baal-peor. The children of Israel entangled themselves into sexual immorality and sensual worshipping of this false god. This demon Belphegor, known to them as Baal-peor entice them into orgies, all types of sexual perversion, and licentiousness.

And Israel abode in Shittim, and the people began to commit whoredom with the daughters of Moab, And they called the people unto the sacrifices of their gods: and the people did eat, and bowed down to their gods. And Israel joined himself unto Baal-peor: and the anger of the Lord was kindled against Israel. And the Lord said unto Moses, take all the heads of the people, and hang them up before the Lord against the sun, that the fierce anger of the Lord may be turned away from Israel. And Moses said unto the judges of Israel, Slay ye every one his men that were joined unto Baal-poer.
Numbers 25:1 - 5

The spirit Belphgor is still in operation in today's society. Disguising his acts in sex slavery which forces women and children into prostitution. Promoting orgies, swingers, menageatrois, gang-rape, and consensual train sex.

The Desert Demon

Azazel is one of the pre-adamic fallen angels who specialize in warfare. This is one of the demons we fight stragically against when we are spiritually warfaring. Azazel is a demon with horns, pointed ears, hairy face, large teeth, long nails, he carries a picture with a banner with a frog on it (in my book, Prayers for Spiritual Warfare, it is noted a frog spirit deals with sexual perversion). He also, stands connected with a goat. In the spirit realm his name is Azazel, but in the earth realm his name is the scapegoat. Azazel is a goat-demon, which promotes women to have sex with goats and maybe other animals. He is also the desert goat that dwells in the desert. He promotes gangwars and his team player is the spirit of divination. In Leviticus 16th chapter, God tells Moses to instruct Aaron to take two goats and present them at the door of the tabernacle of the congregation. Aaron was to cast lots, one for the Lord, and the other lot was for the scapegoat. The scapegoat here represents the idol for Azazel which was sentenced to the wilderness.

> And Aaron shall cast lots upon the two goats: One lot for the Lord, and the other lot for the scapegoat. And Aaron shall bring the goat upon which the Lord's lot fell, and offer him for a sin offering. But the goat, one which the lot fell to be the scapegoat, shall be presented alive before the Lord, to make an atonement with him, and to let him go for a scapegoat into the wilderness.
>
> Leviticus 16:8 - 10

Neither shalt thou lie with any beast to defile thyself therewith: neither shall any woman stand before a beast to lie down thereto: it is confusion. Defile not

ye yourself in any of these things: for in all these the nations are defiled which I cast out before you:
Leviticus 18:23 - 24

Baalzebub

In the Old Testament, Baalzebub was a demon god of Ekron, one of the cities that the Philistines occupied. Baalzebub is known as the "demon lord of flies". He lingers around near death experiences, the critically ill, and around the dying. He summons flies to corpses. In 2 Kings 1st chapter, Ahaziah fell through the screen in his upper chamber and he was injured. Ahaziah sent word to consult with a demon "Baalzebub" regarding his recovery. This angered God, because he consulted with a demon, and God pronounced his death.

And Ahaziah fell down through a lattice in his upper chamber that was in Samaria, and was sick: and he sent messengers, and said unto them, Go, inquire of Baal-zebub the god of Ekron whether I shall recover of this disease.
2 Kings 1:2

In the midst of sickness, tragedies, and terminal illnesses. Some folks have consulted demons through voo-doo and different types of witchcraft, to the point of making a pact with the devil for their healing and recovery. Listen we must trust God and speak His word in faith for our divine healing. Remember He is our Jehovah-Ropher our healer. So, we bind the demon Baalzebub and release Raphel angel of healing or Anuel angel of life, health, and protection. Go farther and seal your prayer with God's word.

Chapter 6
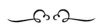

A Prayer for the Spirit of Haman

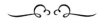

There are ancient demons that has resurrected with an assignment to annihilate family members and nationalities of races and genders. The demon of death Sam(m)uel entered Haman, the Agagite to exterminate a nation of people in the book of Esther. The Jews fasted and prayed for three days, and a race of people was saved.

In the name of Jesus, who took the sting out of death and the victory from the grave. I bind the fallen angel Sam(m)uel who is operating in the strongman Haman, in Jesus Christ, the anointed one name. I cancel your assignment to my bloodline, and my nationality of men, women, boys, and girls. I now destroy your goods: genocide, homicide, suicide, abortion, accidents, domestic violence, and retaliation. I speak now in Jesus name to this demon of death. Be still and return to where you came from. I proclaim the angel Anael spirit of life, protection and health to my bloodline, my nationality of men, women, boys, and girls. I pronounce scriptural weapons against you.

Roman 8:2 For the law of the spirit of life in Christ Jesus hath made _____ free from the law of sin and death.
    (name)

Job 5:20 In famine he shall redeem thee from death; and in war from the power of the sword.

Amen

Pray this prayer for three days, along with serious fasting.

A Prayer for the Incubus or Succubus Spirit

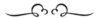

Father, in the name of Jesus Christ, I bind the spirit incubus or succubus that attacks my body and my soulish realm. This demon that's holding my body, my soulish nature and my Id to this unnatural pleasure. I now destroy in Jesus name the origin of this sexual sin created by generational curses of lust, sexual sin, witchcraft and all inherited curses extending back 4 generations. I cancel the assignment of adultery, fornication, molestation, fantasy lust, incest, perversion, homosexuality, pornography, rape, and masturbation caused by the demon incubus or succubus.

I now release in Jesus name, the spirit of holiness and righteousness to my body, soulish realm and my Id. I reject every demon of unnatural pleasure. I activate the word of God in my life.

1 Corinthians 3:16:	Know ye not that my body is the temple of the Holy Ghost. I have been bought with a price: therefore I glorify God in my body and my spirit, which are God's.

Thank you Jesus for total deliverance.

Amen

A Prayer for the Spirit of the Idolater

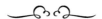

I bind the spirit of Hulda, which promotes the spirit of the idolater which is controlling the soulish realm of _ _____. I break and shatter the stronghold of the
  (name)
pyramid, that is located in the soulish realm; I destroy all manifestations of self gratification such as, selfishness, obsessesion, defensiveness, self centered, protective, possession, carnality, and worshipping of false gods. In Jesus name, I bind the spirit of Hulda and your team players which has exalted itself against the knowledge of God in _____ spirit.
  (name)

I loose the spirit of God the Father, Jesus the Son, and the Holy Spirit to take total residence in _____ life. I now activate this prayer   (name)
with your word: "Thy shalt love the Lord thy God with all thine heart, and with all thy soul, and with all thy might".
                      Deuteronomy 6:5

  In the name of Jesus Christ, the anointed one.
                                    Amen

A Prayer for Homosexuality

Father God, in Jesus name. I bind the demonic spirit Cerevello which has been assigned to the spirit nature of _____.
(name)
This spirit that has promoted homosexuality within my bloodline. I now repent for every sexual sin within my bloodline extending back to four generations. Asking you Lord Jesus to forgive my family tree. I spoil unnatural affection, same sex relationship, transformation of sexual gender, and bisexual involvement. I also spoil the spirit of Heaviness, suicidal tendency and rejection. I spoil every manifestation of Cerevello which has attacked the spirit nature of the man _____ _____ or the woman _____ in Jesus name.
(name) (name)

I loose his or her spirit to be free according to the way God has created _____. I now activate the word to
(name)
come alive in _____ life. Now the Lord is that
(name)
spirit, and where the spirit of the Lord is, there is liberty.

God I proclaim _____ spirit will be filled with
(name)

the Holy Spirit, the word of God, and the fruit of the spirit, in Jesus name.

Amen

The Spirit of Heaviness

Father God, in the name of Jesus Christ our Savior, the anointed one. I bind the strongman, spirit of heaviness, that has attacked the soulish realm of _____ in
(name)
Jesus name. I spoil every demonic manifestation depression, sadness, suicide, sorrow, grief, discouragement, bruised, and despair that has resident within the emotions of emotions _____ soulish realm. I now wash _____
(name)   (name)
with Jesus shed blood.

I loose now the oil of Joy and the garment of praise to _____ emotion. I now seal this prayer with the word
(name)
of God: "the spirit of the Lord God is upon to comfort that mourn, to give unto beauty for ashes, the oil of joy for mourning, the garment of praise for the spirit of heaviness".
Isaiah 61:1-3

Amen

Sexual Perversion rooted in the Id

Father God, in Jesus anointed name, I bind the spirit of sexual perversion that has arrested the id portion of my personality. Which has bound me to inappropriate instant sexual gratification. Jesus, allow the anointing to destroy all yokes of pornography, homosexuality, pedophiles, prostitution, fornication, adultery, filthy mind, incest, rape, error, rebellion, and lust. I uproot these manifestations from my soulish realm targeting my mind, emotion, and imagination. I uproot it from my id and body desires in Jesus name. Lord sanctify me according to your word. In whom also "ye are circumcised with the circumcision made without hands in putting off the body of the sins of the flesh by the circumcision of Christ".

Colossians 2:11

A Prayer against the Spirit of Hulda

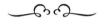

In the name of Jesus I bind and decapitate the demon spirit of hulda. I render your assignment helpless and hopeless. You will no longer place demonic spirits into the creatures of the night, such as owls, snakes, bats, frogs, in demon objects, and idols. I will no longer admire or worship these idols which are possessed by demonic forces. Lord Jesus, I repent of allowing these idols to resident within my home.

I now loose the Holy Spirit, the third God head of the Holy trinity to take domain in my home, my office, and all my dwelling in Jesus name. I now activate this prayer with your holy word: "thou shalt have none other gods before me".

*For house cleaning read my book "Prayers for Spiritual Warfare", requiring removing creatures of the night.

A Personal Prayer for the Spirit of Infirmity

In the name of Jesus Christ, I _____, bind the strongman (name) infirmity in Jesus name. I also bind every generational curse of infirmity extending back to four generations both on my father and mother's bloodline. In Jesus name I speak death to every manifestation of diseases such as cancer, lupus, HIV, and every other abnormal process within my body. None of these things shall consume me or overtake me. I stand on the promise. God you said you would bless the seed of my mother's womb. I am my mother's seed and God you sent your word and healed me from all my destructions. Thank you God, for my divine healing in Jesus name. I now seal this prayer with your omnipotent word: "who forgiveth all thine iniquities: who healeth all thy diseases".

Thank you Lord Jesus for this dimensional miracle.

                                                                     Amen

A Prayer for the Spirit of Infirmity (Cancer)

Father God, in your son Jesus name, I claim the promises of your word. Your word said, man shall not live by bread alone, but by every word that proceed out of your mouth. Your word, which can not return void, but it must prosper in the thing it was sent to. Your word said; the just shall live by faith. I am the just. Now I speak in faith. I bind this spirit of infimity now. I spoil and remove every manifestation of cancer in my colon, my bones, and every organ in my body in the name of Jesus Christ. I loose divine healing to me now. Right now in Jesus name. I now activate Now Faith in my body in Jesus name. I seal this prayer with your healing words:

> "But he was wounded for our transgression, he was bruised for our iniquities: the chastisement of our peace was upon him; and with his stripes I am healed".
>
> Isaiah 53:5

Heal me, O Lord, and I shall be healed: save me, and I shall be saved: for thou are my praise.

Thank you Jesus for my divine healing. Thank you for this dimensional miracle.

Testimony: (By one of the disciple's in ministry) I was diagnosed with cancer, the doctors didn't give me much of a chance. The doctor said that it was nothing they could do. My Apostle and Elders of the Tree of Life Deliverance Ministry, prayed for me. My Apostle designed this special prayer of faith which I had to read three times a day. After taking further tests my doctor couldn't find any traces of cancer, Amen! To God Be the Glory. (07/08)

Amen

*Read three times a Day

GLOSSARY

Bestiality - A sexual act between a human and an animal.

Dunamis - A Greek word which means power.

Effeminate - A male that demonstrates female characteristics.

Spirit of Hulda - Demon spirit that promotes demonic activity in inadement objects.

Incubus - A male sexual demon that seeks sexual intercourse with females. This spirit targets her body, soul, and the ID.

Spirit of Korah - Demonic spirit in ministry that promotes rebellion against spiritual authority.

Spirit of Leviathan - A demon spirit that attacks the soulish realm of man, promoting pride and distraction.

Spirit of Mammon - A demon that provokes a love for money and greed.

Spirit of Manasseh - A warlock demon, that promotes desecration of the church and invokes child sacrifice.

Mitochondria - The power source of cells.

Spirit of Orion - A demon spirit that targets deliverance ministers and deliverance churches.

Spirit of Sam(m)uel - Demon spirit of death.

Succubus - A female sexual demon that seeks intercourse with males. This spirit targets his body, soul, and Id.

Printed in the United States
207868BV00001B/301-1176/P